The text of Genesis 1:1-2:4a was especially translated
from the Hebrew text (as edited by Rudolf Kittel) for
use in this book.

THE STORY OF CREATION

Genesis 1:1-2:4a

Illustrated by Holly and Ivar Zapp

Logos International
Plainfield, New Jersey

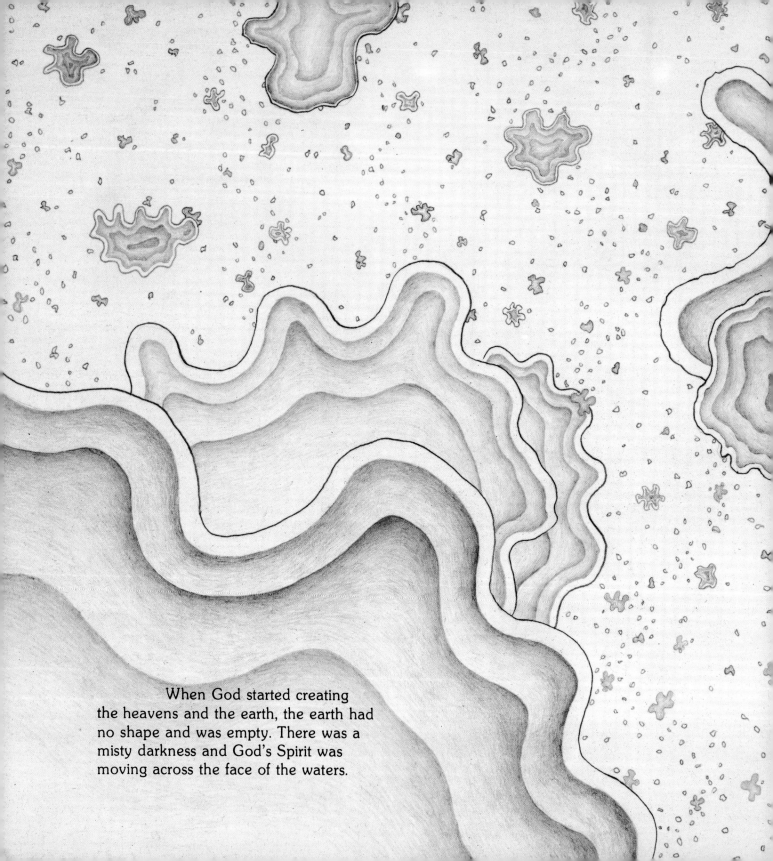

When God started creating
the heavens and the earth, the earth had
no shape and was empty. There was a
misty darkness and God's Spirit was
moving across the face of the waters.

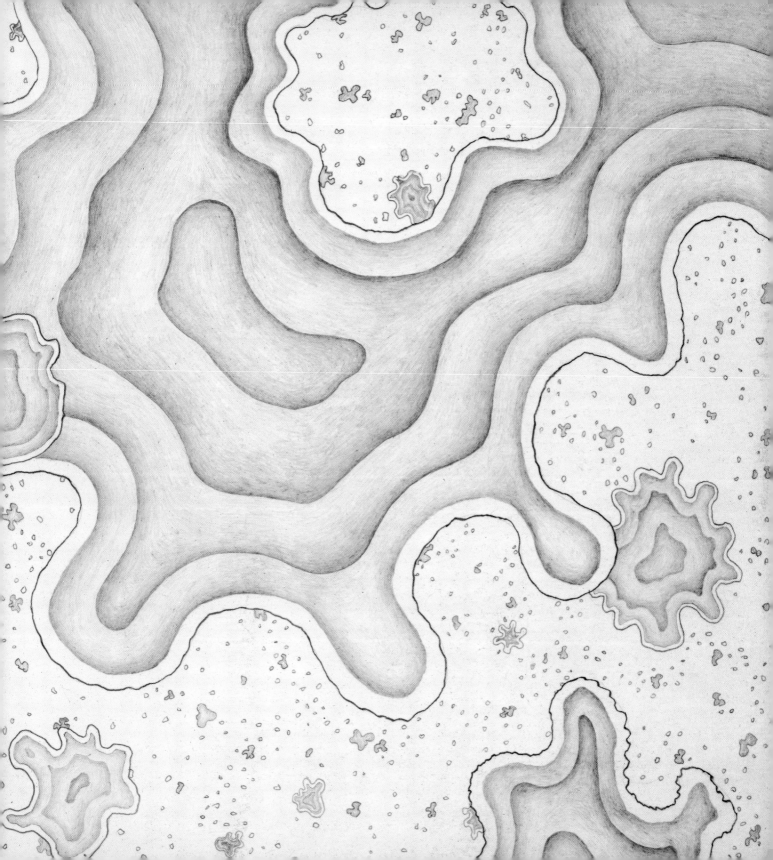

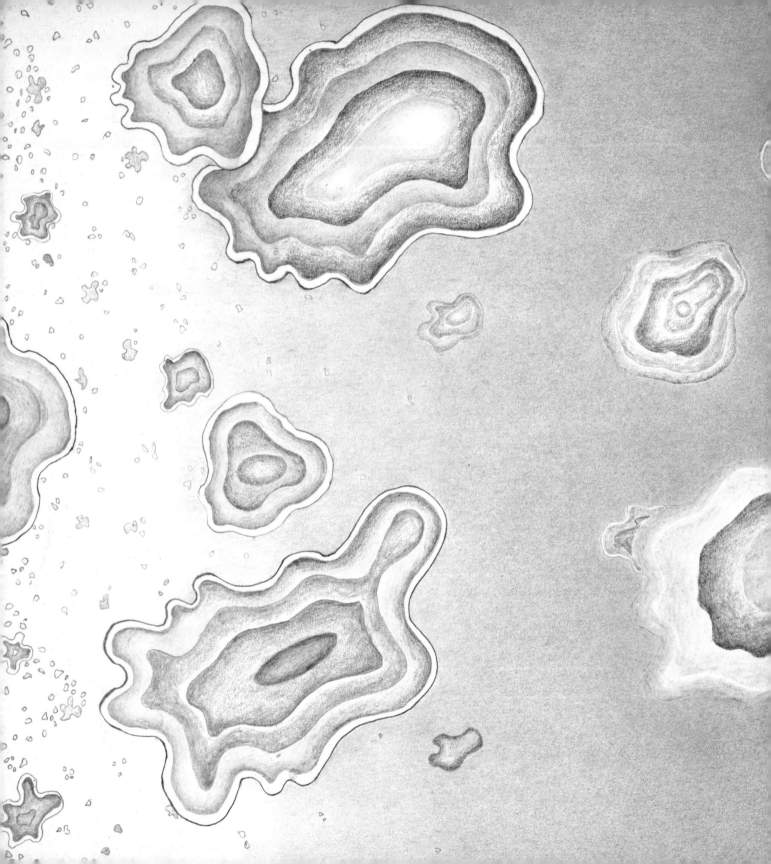

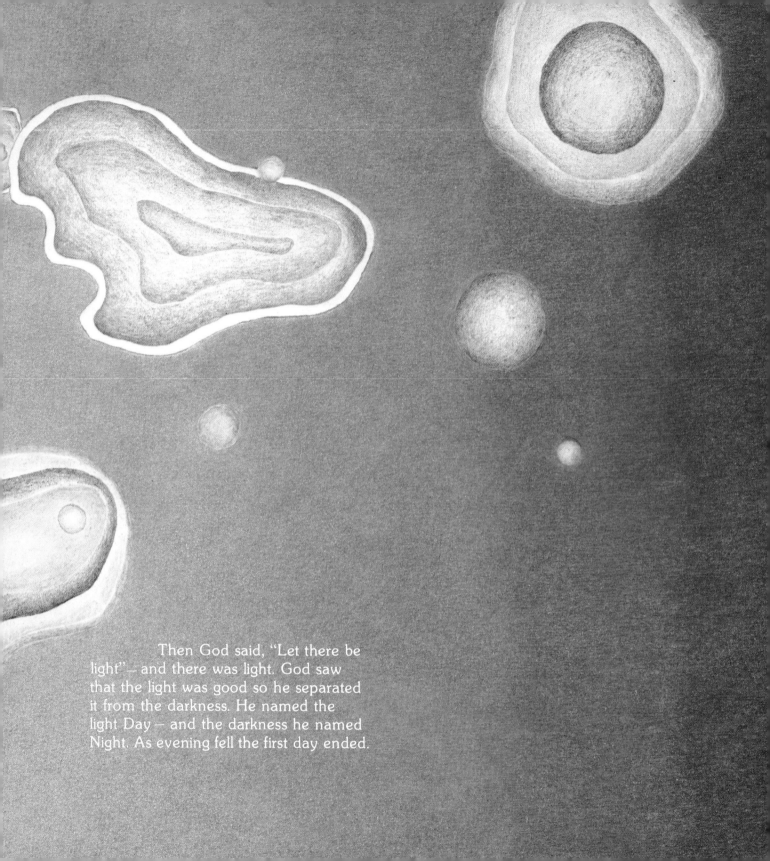

Then God said, "Let there be light"—and there was light. God saw that the light was good so he separated it from the darkness. He named the light Day—and the darkness he named Night. As evening fell the first day ended.

In the morning God said, "Let there be a great covering between the waters to set them apart from each other." God made that covering and set the waters under it apart from the waters above it—and it was done. He named the covering Heaven. As evening fell the second day ended.

The next morning God said,
"Let the waters under Heaven be
gathered together into one place, and let
dry land appear." And so it was. God
named the dry land Earth. The gathered
waters God called Seas. And God saw
that it was good. Then he said, "Let
the earth produce green growing things,
plants bearing their own seed, and fruit
trees bearing fruit with their own kinds of
seeds inside them, all over the earth"—
and so it was. The earth did exactly
as God had said. God saw that it was
good, and as evening fell the third
day ended.

The next morning God said, "Let there be lights in the covering of heaven to divide day from night, and let them be for signs and for seasons and for days and years, and let them be lights in the covering of heaven to shine down on the earth." And so it was. God made the two great lights, the sun to rule the day and the moon to rule the night. He also made the stars. God put them in the covering of heaven to shine on the earth, to rule the day and the night, and to set light apart from darkness. God saw that it was good; evening came and the fourth day ended.

On the morning of the fifth day God said, "Let the waters swarm with living creatures, and let the birds fly above the earth within the covering of heaven."

So God created the great sea monsters and every living creature that swarms in the waters, according to their kinds, and also every kind of thing that flies with wings. And he saw that it was good. God blessed them, saying "Be fruitful, multiply, and fill the waters of the seas—and let birds multiply all over the earth." Evening fell and the fifth day drew to a close.

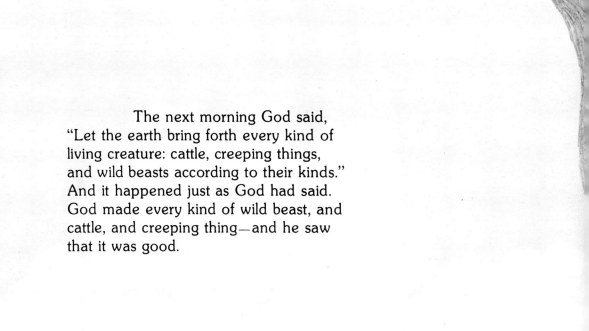

The next morning God said,
"Let the earth bring forth every kind of
living creature: cattle, creeping things,
and wild beasts according to their kinds."
And it happened just as God had said.
God made every kind of wild beast, and
cattle, and creeping thing—and he saw
that it was good.

Then God said, "Let us make
all men in our image, in our own likeness,
and let them be masters of the fish of
the sea, the birds of the air, the cattle, the
whole earth—even the creeping things
that creep upon the earth."

God created man in his own image,
in the image of God he created him,
male and female he created them.

And God blessed them saying, "Be fruitful and multiply, fill the earth and conquer it. Be masters of the fish of the sea, the birds of the air, and every living thing that moves upon the earth." God said, "See, I have given you all the seed-bearing plants in the whole world, and all the trees with seed-bearing fruit; they are yours for food. I give the green plants for food to all the animals, birds, and creeping things—every creature that breathes air." And so it was. God saw everything he had made—it was very good. Evening came and the sixth day ended.

That is how the heavens and
the earth were completed with all the
things that go with them. On the morning
of the seventh day God's work was all
finished and on that day he rested.
So God blessed the seventh day and
made it holy, because on that day he
rested after all his work of creating.
   This is how the heavens and
the earth began when they were created.

This book was set in twelve point Souvenir type on fourteen points of lead in Plainfield, New Jersey.